英語長文問題

CROSSOVER

1

Daiichi Gakushusha

本書の使い方
HOW TO USE CROSSOVER

本文の語数と, 本文を読むための目標時間です。

すべての問題を解くための制限時間です。

本文に関連する教科やSDGsを示します。英文を読む力に加え, 他の教科等や社会の諸問題に関する知見を深める問題集です。

レッスンは難易度順に配列しました。
CROSSOVER ①では
250〜400語の英文を中心に収録しています。

英文の選定基準
・他の教科等で学習する内容を含むもの
・SDGsの17の目標に深く関連したもの
・現代的な話題

CROSSOVER ①では
CEFR-A1レベルを到達目標に設定し,
本文は**CEFR-A1レベル**の文法で構成しました。

脚注の二次元コードから, 本文の音声を聞くことができます。
・情報料は無料ですが, 通信費は利用者の負担となります。
・本書の発行終了とともに上記コンテンツの配信を終了することがあります。

英文を読みやすくするため, 脚注では語の注釈を多めに取り上げています。
覚えるべき語句として, 別冊『多読と整理』で同じ語句を取り上げている場合もあります。

Lesson 8

語数(速読目標時間)	関連教科	関連 SDGs	得 点
296(3分)	情報	—	/50
制限時間			
20分			

1 Let me share two important points to help you know *whether the information is correct or not.

2 First of all, it is important to give up the thought that "a search will answer all of the questions in the world." There are many other sources of information in the world besides the Internet. *Instead of trying to solve all your questions with information from the Internet, it is better to use the Internet as a *supplement or a starting point for your research. If you do not use the Internet with such an attitude, false information may *deceive you easily. If you do not go to the library or contact an expert, you will not learn really important things.

3 It is (1)also important to have (2)the ability to read and understand long texts. If you do not have the ability to read long texts, you will not be able to understand what is written in them. (3)You will be *overwhelmed by their large number of words and regard the texts as true just because they are written in long sentences. A large amount of text does not always mean that the truth is written correctly and in detail. When AI technology is used, it is possible to create long sentences with little *substance. A long text may seem *plausible at first. When you read carefully, however, it often *turns out to be a long text that *makes no sense at all. It is necessary to improve your reading skill by practicing reading books.

4 Keep (4)these two points in mind and you will be able to avoid misinformation. If you under... ...e amount...

whether ... or not：…かどうか　　instead of ...：…のかわりに，…ではなく　　supplement：補足　　deceive：…をだます
overwhelm：…を圧倒する　　substance：内容，中身　　plausible：もっともらしい
turn out to be ...：…であるとわかる　　make sense：意味をなす

別冊『多読と整理』の使い方
HOW TO USE THE ANNEX

■多読

別冊は見開き構成で, 左ページは
「本文と同じテーマの別英文とその設問」で構成しています。
SNS・レシピ・記事など, さまざまなテキストタイプの英文を読むことができます。
本文を読む前の背景知識の習得や,
本文を読んだ後の追加演習として使うことができます。

設問に解答するために必要な力を「タグ」として示しました。

- 🖙 知識・技能：語彙・文法・句読法などに関わる問題です。
- 🖙 主題：文章全体や段落の主題を把握する問題です。速読スキルを身に付けることができます。
- 🖙 文章展開：段落どうしのつながりに関わる問題です。
- 🖙 段落構成：一つの段落の構成などに関わる問題です。パラグラフ・ライティングの参考にすることもできます。
- 🖙 論理：ディスコースマーカーなどの文脈や，どうしてそう言えるのかを問う問題です。

※その他，問題に応じたタグを付けています。

1. Which of the following is the main point of paragraph 2?　🖙 主題 (7 点)
   a. Going to the library and contacting an expert is better than searching on the Internet.
   b. Information from the Internet is always false.
   c. Information from the Internet is not always correct.
   d. You can find all you need to know through the Internet.

2. In paragraph 3, (1)also is used to ☐.　🖙 文章展開 (7 点)
   a. introduce the writer's second important point
   b. show that both readers and the writer have to have the ability to read a long text
   c. say that information from the Internet and other sources is true
   d. suggest that reading both short and long texts is important

3. Why do you have to have (2)the ability to read and understand long texts?　In order to have it, what does the writer want you to do?　Explain in Japanese.　🖙 段落構成 (各 7 点)

なぜ必要か：＿＿＿＿＿＿＿＿＿＿＿＿＿＿＿＿＿＿＿＿

筆者は何をしてほしいと思っているか：＿＿＿＿＿＿＿＿＿＿＿
＿＿＿＿＿＿＿＿＿＿＿＿＿＿＿＿＿＿＿＿＿＿＿＿＿＿

設問文は英語で記されています。
よく使われる表現を確認しておきましょう。

According to the text, ...「本文によると，…。」
　→本文にない内容を答えないようにしましょう。
Be sure to make ... clear.「…を明確にしなさい。」
　→…には指示表現などが入ります。指示表現の内容を明確にして答えましょう。
Explain in detail ....「詳しく説明しなさい。」
　→支持文の内容なども交えて，できるだけ詳細に答えましょう。
Translate the following into Japanese: ....「…以下を日本語に翻訳しなさい。」
　→なるべく自然な日本語になるよう心がけましょう。
You may choose more than one option.「選択肢を二つ以上選んでもよい。」
　→複数解答が正答になる可能性があります。

設問の工夫

- ・選択式と記述式のバランスに留意しました。
  ※記述式は日本語記述が中心です。
- ・筆者の意図や，「なぜこの語を使ったか」を問う問題を採用しました。
  ※モデルとなる本文を多く読むことで，「書く」技能を向上させることもできます。
- ・本文と日常生活をリンクさせて解答する問題を採用しました。
- ・選択式では，消去法が最適の解法となる問題を可能なかぎり避けました。
- ・文法的な正しさや，用語や用法の区別が中心となる問題を避けました。
- ・和訳問題や，該当箇所を和訳することで答える問題を少なくしました。
  ※ 🖙 知識・技能 タグの問題は和訳問題が中心です。

「解答・解説集」で，選択式の「誤りの選択肢」の根拠や，記述式の「答案例と採点基準」などを示しています。

■整理
右ページは「本文の設問の解答欄」「語句の意味調べ」「要約完成」で構成しています。
本文の設問の解答欄
語句の意味調べ：意味を知っておくべき単語をピックアップしました。取り上げられた単語や表現の意味を書いて覚えましょう（本文の脚注で同じ語句を扱っている場合があります）。
要約完成：本文の概要を理解できたか，要約完成で確認しましょう。ここでは空所補充形式としていますが，慣れてきたら自分で本文を要約し，ストーリーリテリングにも挑戦してみましょう。

CONTENTS

語数	関連教科	関連SDGs
270語	国語	

語数	関連教科	関連SDGs
298語	地理歴史	

語数	関連教科	関連SDGs
254語	公民	5 GENDER EQUALITY / 8 DECENT WORK AND ECONOMIC GROWTH

語数	関連教科	関連SDGs
310語	理科	15 LIFE ON LAND

語数	関連教科	関連SDGs
272語		14 LIFE BELOW WATER

語数	関連教科	関連SDGs
256語	保健体育	2 ZERO HUNGER / 3 GOOD HEALTH AND WELL-BEING

語数	関連教科	関連SDGs
281語	外国語	

語数	関連教科	関連SDGs
296語	情報	

語数	関連教科	関連SDGs
302語	家庭	1 NO POVERTY / 2 ZERO HUNGER

The following is an essay written by a Japanese student who is researching the history of words.

1 According to one survey, more than 90% of 16- to 19-year-olds use the Japanese word "yabai" with the positive meaning of "wonderful" *in addition to its original bad meaning. More than half of those in their 30s and younger use the word in the same way. On the other hand, those in their 40s and older tend not to use the word "yabai" with a positive meaning. (1)This *indicates that the meaning of the word "yabai" is changing.

2 Some people say that the meaning of a word should change with the time and cultural changes. (2)Not only in Japanese, but also in English, there are words whose meanings have changed. For example, the word "nice" originally meant "stupid." However, it *came to be used with its *current positive meaning around the 19th century. Similarly, it is natural for the younger generation to use the word "yabai" with a different meaning.

3 (3)On the other hand, there are some people who *point out the negative effects of such changes on *intergenerational communication. Language is an important tool for communication, so using the word with meanings that are not familiar to some people may *hinder communication. (4)Learning, understanding, and correctly using the original meaning of words is important because several generations live together in our society.

4 What do you think? I think it is not a bad thing that the meanings of words change as time goes by. However, I do not think it is a good idea to use only one word, "yabai," to *describe any situation in our daily life. Other words will often describe the situation much better than "yabai."

---

in addition to ...：…に加えて　　indicate：…を示す　　come to ～：～するようになる　　current：現在の
point out ...：…を指摘する　　intergenerational：世代を超えた　　hinder：…を妨げる，阻害する
describe：…を描写する

1. As you can see in the example of the Japanese word "yabai," ☐. 主題 （7点）

    a. a word sometimes comes to have quite different meanings

    b. many Japanese people are losing their vocabulary

    c. the change of the meaning of a word often becomes a social problem

    d. the younger generation tends to use words with a positive meaning

2. What is (1)this? Explain in detail in Japanese.   指示語 （10点）

_____

_____

3. Translate the following into Japanese: (2)Not only in Japanese, but also in English, there are words whose meanings have changed.   知識・技能 （9点）

_____

_____

4. (3)On the other hand is used for ☐.   文章展開 （7点）

    a. adding more information to support the opinion written before it

    b. giving some examples of the change in the meaning of words

    c. introducing an opinion with the different point of view

    d. showing that the writer disagrees with the idea written before it

5. Why do some people say (4)learning, understanding, and correctly using the original meaning of words is important because several generations live together in our society? Explain in detail in Japanese.   論理 （10点）

_____

_____

6. Which best summarizes the writer's opinion about the topic?   全体把握 （7点）

    a. It is useful that we can show several feelings with one word.

    b. Sometimes "yabai" describes a situation much better.

    c. We should not depend too much on the word "yabai" in our daily life.

    d. We should stop intergenerational communication.

❶ Do you like chocolate? Most people love it. Its sweet, creamy *flavor is hard to *resist. But where did chocolate come from?

❷ About 2,600 years ago, *the Olmec, an ancient group in Central and South America, *made use of chocolate. They used cocoa beans to make a special drink, but this drink was not sweet like the chocolate we eat. It was very bitter. In the years that followed, they started adding other things to their cocoa drink to make it taste better.

❸ Chocolate was very important for *the Maya, another group in Central America. The Mayans used cocoa beans as money. For example, 10 beans could buy a rabbit. Cocoa beans were also used in Mayan *religion and wedding ceremonies. The Mayans also used cocoa beans to make a chocolate drink, but only rich people *could afford to drink it.

❹ When the Europeans arrived in South America, they started to take (1)this popular drink back to their home countries. Milk, cream, and sugar were added, and eventually the chocolate we know was born. In the year 1689, chocolate milk was developed in Jamaica.

❺ (2)Chocolate is now one of the most popular flavors in the world. In modern society, we can enjoy chocolate in bars, ice cream, cakes, milkshakes, pies, and many other foods. Some studies have found that dark chocolate is good for our health because it benefits the *circulatory system and has other *anticancer properties. (3)Thus, small but regular amounts of dark chocolate might be able to reduce the risk of a heart attack.

❻ (4)Nothing is perfect, and chocolate is no *exception. Chocolate can contain a large amount of calories, so people who eat a lot of chocolate may become fat. Perhaps the secret to enjoying chocolate's flavor and not *ruining your health is very simple: ☐ X ☐!

---

flavor：風味，味　　resist：(好きなものを)がまんする　　the Olmec：オルメカ族　　make use of ...：…を利用する
the Maya：マヤ族　　religion：宗教　　can afford to ～：～する余裕がある
circulatory system：循環系統(血液がめぐる体のシステム)　　anticancer property：抗がん作用　　exception：例外
ruin：…を台なしにする，損なう

本文音声

1. According to the text, cocoa beans were ☐. キーワード（7点）

  a. added to the bitter drink the Olmec loved

  b. brought back to European countries after Jamaicans developed chocolate milk

  c. the main trading item between European countries and South American countries

  d. used by Mayans to buy things

2. What does (1)this popular drink mean? Write an English phrase of three words.

指示表現 （8点）

_____

3. The writer begins paragraph 5 by saying (2)chocolate is now one of the most popular flavors in the world in order to ☐. 文章展開 （7点）

  a. give some examples of chocolate-flavored foods

  b. help readers notice that the paragraph is explaining the present, not the past

  c. inform the readers that the chocolate can transform its appearance

  d. show respect for the person who developed chocolate for the first time

4. Translate the following into Japanese: (3)Thus, small but regular amounts of dark chocolate might be able to reduce the risk of a heart attack. 知識・技能 （10点）

_____

_____

5. What does the writer want to tell by saying (4)nothing is perfect, and chocolate is no exception? Explain in detail in Japanese. 段落構成 （10点）

_____

_____

6. Write an English phrase or a sentence that suits for ☐ X ☐. 知識・技能 文章展開 （8点）

_____

Lesson
3

語数（速読目標時間）	関連教科	関連SDGs		得　点
254（2分30秒）	公民			
制限時間				
20分				/ 50

1 Smokejumpers are a special type of firefighter. They jump from planes or are *lowered by helicopters into areas that are difficult to reach by car or on foot, such as the middle of a mountain forest. They race to *put out fires as fast as they can.

5 **2** At a fire site, smokejumpers first *examine the land and decide how to fight the fire. (1)Their main goal is to stop the fire from spreading or to slow its *progress until the ground-based firefighters arrive. By using basic equipment such as shovels and axes, the smokejumpers *clear the land of *burnable material, such as dry grass and dead trees. They carry water with them, too, but 10 only a limited amount.

3 (2)Although the *majority of smokejumpers are men, more women are joining now. The most important factors are their height and weight. For example, smokejumpers employed in the United States must be between 120 and 200 pounds (between 54 and 91 kilograms) so they don't get *blown over 15 by the strong winds or get hurt when they *land. Smokejumpers must also be able to survive in the *wilderness. In Russia, many smokejumpers know how to find food in the forest and can even make simple *furniture from trees.

4 The work is dangerous, and the hours are long. But for these firefighters, (3)smokejumping isn't just an *occupation. They love being able to jump out of 20 planes, fight fires, and live in the forest. As 28-year-old Russian smokejumper Alexi Tishin says, "(4)This is the best job for tough guys."

---

lower：…をおろす，下げる　　put out ...：…を消す　　examine：…を調査する　　progress：進行
clear A of B：AからBを取りのぞく　　burnable：可燃性の　　majority：大多数　　blow ... over：…を（風で）吹き飛ばす
land：着地する　　wilderness：荒地　　furniture：家具　　occupation：職業

本文音声

1. Smokejumpers are different from ordinary firefighters because ☐. ✎ 主題 (7点)

   a. they don't bring water with them to the scene of a fire

   b. they give instructions to fight a fire from planes or helicopters

   c. they try to put out a fire as fast as possible

   d. they use very simple tools to fight a fire

2. Suppose that you want to become a smokejumper. It might be difficult to make your dream come true if ☐. ✎ 内容理解 (7点)

   a. you do not have any experiences as a firefighter

   b. you do not have knowledge or skills to survive in the forest

   c. you do not live in the United States

   d. your height and weight are appropriate for the job

3. Translate the following into Japanese: (1)Their main goal is to stop the fire from spreading or to slow its progress until the ground-based firefighters arrive.

✎ 知識・技能 (10点)

_____

_____

4. Why does the writer say (2)although the majority of smokejumpers are men, more women are joining now? Choose the best option. ✎ 論理 (10点)

   a. スモークジャンパーになるための条件に，性別が無関係であることを示すため。

   b. スモークジャンパーの大半は男性であることを示すため。

   c. 女性にスモークジャンパーになってほしいことを示すため。

   d. 女性の方がスモークジャンパーに向いていることを示すため。

5. Which of the following best describes (3)smokejumping isn't just an occupation?

   a. Smokejumpers don't want to do their job but they have to. ✎ 論理 (7点)

   b. Smokejumpers regard their job as the best occupation of the world.

   c. For smokejumpers, the job is more than about earning money.

   d. The job requires much more than it pays.

6. Why did Alexi Tishin use the word "tough" in (4)this is the best job for tough guys?

✎ 意見 (9点)

_____

Lesson

4

語数（速読目標時間）	関連教科	関連 SDGs	得 点
310（3分）	理科	 15 LIFE ON LAND	
制限時間			
20分			/ 50

1 We all remember stories about *wolves from our childhood. Perhaps you feel they have some mysterious powers, or perhaps you are afraid of them. Throughout history, (1)these animals have been hunted, and the number of wolves living in the wild has dropped. But, in recent years, people have started

5 to try to increase the number of wolves. In countries that have lost wolves completely, they have tried to bring them back from *extinction. Why?

2 Animals like wolves and bears are top *predators. They have an important role in *eco-systems. Without them, populations of animals like *deer just grow and grow, and (2)this causes serious problems. In Japan, for example, huge

10 populations of deer are causing *crop damage, *soil erosion, and car accidents. Deer can also carry disease.

3 In parts of Europe and the US, environmental experts have *encouraged wolf populations to grow and spread. They have tried (3)to "rewild" certain areas. This process has successfully reduced the number of deer and other animals

15 which eat or damage young trees. Thanks to this, forests have grown back and their natural eco-systems have begun to work *properly. This means (4)we can have clean air and water in the future and *cope better with climate change.

4 Nature is important for our physical and mental health. Many people hope this rewilding will create *opportunities for people to *reconnect with nature as

20 they visit these wild spaces. This nature tourism also helps the economy in rural areas. But not everyone supports the idea of bringing back wolves. Farmers, especially *sheep farmers, worry that wolves will kill their baby sheep. Many people are scared of wolves and don't like the idea.

5 In fact, wolf attacks on people are very rare. And, rewilding is an effective,

25 long-term, and low-cost solution to some of the serious environmental issues we face. (5)We need to learn to live with wolves.

---

wolf：オオカミ　　extinction：絶滅　　predator：捕食者　　eco-system：生態系　　deer：シカ　　crop：農作物
soil erosion：土壌侵食　　encourage ... to ～：…に～するよう促す　　properly：適切に　　cope with ...：…に対処する
opportunity：機会　　reconnect：再びつながる　　sheep：羊

 本文音声

1. The writer would agree with the idea that ☐.　　　　　　　　　　✎ 主題 （7点）

   a. increasing the number of wolves is good though some people may not agree

   b. the actions to increase the number of wolves will not succeed

   c. wolves spread disease because they eat deer

   d. young trees will be lost because wolves eat or attack them

2. Translate the following into Japanese: (1)these animals have been hunted, and the number of wolves living in the wild has dropped.　Be sure to make "these animals" clear.　　　　　　　　　　✎ 知識・技能 （8点）

_____

_____

3. What does (2)this causes serious problems mean?　Explain in detail in Japanese.　Be sure to make "this" clear and give some examples of "serious problems."　✎ 段落構成 （9点）

_____

_____

4. Which of the following has the similar meaning to (3)to "rewild" certain areas?

   a. to leave forests as they are without taking any action　　✎ 知識・技能 （7点）

   b. to leave urban cities and start living in forests

   c. to release wolves into forest areas　　d. to stop taking care of animals

5. The writer thinks that (4)we can have clean air and water in the future and cope better with climate change if the population of wolves increases.　Why?　Put the correct phrases below in the blanks.　　　　　　　　　　✎ 論理 （各2点）

> Forests do not grow because ⑤① .　However, if ② , ③ .　It helps ④ .　Since ⑤ , the writer says, "we can have clean air and water in the future, and cope better with climate change."

   a. deer often carry disease　　b. not everyone supports the idea of bringing back wolves

   c. some animals often eat or damage young trees　　d. the number of these animals will drop

   e. they play an important role in solving environmental problems

   f. wolves eat the animals　　g. young trees in forests grow

6. Why does the writer think (5)we need to learn to live with wolves?　Explain in Japanese.　　　　　　　　　　✎ 文章展開 （9点）

_____

語数（速読目標時間）	関連教科	関連SDGs	得 点
272（2分40秒）	—	14 LIFE BELOW WATER	
制限時間			
20分			/ 50

1 The world's oceans and rivers are home to many *species of fish, shellfish and other sea creatures. People have been consuming them to feed their families and to maintain their communities. (1)Since ancient times, seafood and human society have been closely connected.

2 Today, however, the populations of marine and river wildlife are *declining. One of the reasons for this is the growth of the world's human population. As the number of people becomes larger, we need more seafood. (2)Technological advances that make fishing more efficient have also contributed to the decline. Every year, more than 77 billion kilograms of wildlife are removed from the ocean. Scientists fear that the world's fishing industry will *collapse in the near future if this trend continues.

3 Under these *circumstances, "(3)sustainable fishing" is becoming increasingly important. It is a set of *practices that prevents *overfishing. Fishing while protecting marine life means that we will have access to marine resources *for many years to come. It also leads to the *preservation of *employment for people who are involved in the fishing industry. Sustainable fishing is essential not only for marine life, but also (4)for our future generations.

4 Here is an example of sustainable fishing. (5)*The Tagbanua people in the Philippines have traditionally used fishing methods that maintain the fish populations. They fish for specific species only during specific times of the year. In this way, the fish populations are kept from declining. They also *designate certain areas as protected areas, and no one can catch fish there. When fishing, traditional fishers use simple hooks and lines to catch only the amount they need for themselves and their communities.

---

species：種　　decline：減少する　　collapse：崩壊する　　circumstance：状況　　practice：取り組み，実践
overfishing：過剰漁業，乱獲　　for many years to come：将来にわたって　　preservation：維持
employment：雇用　　the Tagbanua：タグバヌア族（フィリピンの先住民族）　　designate：…を指定する

 本文音声

1. Which of the following has the closest meaning to (1)since ancient times, seafood and human society have been closely connected? 段落構成 (7点)

a. Human beings lived in the ocean, so seafood species are our relatives.

b. Humans have survived for thousands of years thanks to seafood.

c. People have loved eating seafood for a long time.

d. Seafood and human beings have been sharing similar features.

2. Translate the following into Japanese: (2)Technological advances that make fishing more efficient have also contributed to the decline. 知識・技能 (9点)

_____

3. Choose the most appropriate example of (3)sustainable fishing from the following. 主題 (7点)

a. Catching a large amount of fish so that everyone can have it without inequality.

b. Developing technologies that can bring extinct fish back to life.

c. Limiting the amount of fish we catch to maintain the population of marine life.

d. Reducing the number of people who work in the fishing industry.

4. Why is sustainable fishing essential (4)for our future generations? Explain two reasons in Japanese. 段落構成 (各6点)

- _____
- _____

5. Which of the following is **not** true about (5)the Tagbanua people? 内容理解 (7点)

a. They have been using the same fishing methods and tools for a long time.

b. They have changed their fishing methods to maintain the fish populations.

c. They never fish in prohibited areas.   d. They try not to catch too many fish.

6. According to the article, which two of the following statements are true? Choose two options. The order does not matter. 全体把握 (各4点)

a. According to the scientists, the fishing industry is in danger of collapse.

b. Fishing in traditional ways is always good for marine life.

c. Preventing overfishing has benefits for both marine wildlife and our future children.

d. As the human population becomes larger, we eat less seafood.

1 When people think of (1)problems related to *nutrition in the developing world, they probably think of hunger.　But in low- and middle-*income countries, the number of young people who are *overweight is *catching up with the number who are underweight.　In 1975, overweight children were
5　almost unknown outside the developed countries. Just 0.3% of people aged 5 to 19 years in developing countries were suffering from *obesity.　That *figure has risen to 7% today.　Meanwhile, the number of children who are *defined as underweight in low- and middle-income countries has decreased, from 13% to 10%.　According to the WHO, if current trends continue, the number of
10　overweight children worldwide will become larger than that of *undernourished children in the near future.

2 You might think it is strange that countries can have high levels both of hunger and of obesity.　But (2)the two are linked.　Poor parents tend to look for the most *affordable meals to fill up their children.　Thanks to the spread of
15　convenience foods and *energy-dense processed carbohydrates, the cheapest foods often deliver extremely little nutrition while they *contain too many calories.　(3)That puts children who eat a lot of them at risk of obesity.

3 ┌─────── X ───────┐, in some countries, although the number of their underweight children is falling sharply, another problem is happening.　For example, South
20　Africa cut the share of its children who are underweight from about 20% in 1975 to less than 5% today.　Over the same period, its childhood obesity rate went from about zero to more than 10%.

---

nutrition：栄養　　income：収入　　overweight：太りすぎの ↔ underweight：やせすぎの
catch up with ...：…に追いつく　　obesity：肥満　　figure：数値　　define A as B：AをBと定義する
undernourished：栄養不良の　　affordable：価格が手ごろな
energy-dense processed carbohydrates：高エネルギーの加工炭水化物食品　　contain：…を含む

本文音声

1. Which of the (1)problems related to nutrition in the developing world is mainly written in this text? Explain in about 30 words in Japanese. ✑主題（7点）

_____

2. Which graph best describes paragraph 1 ?　✑情報整理（7点）

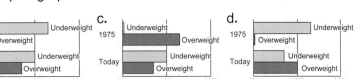

3. As to (2)the two are linked, what are "the two"? Why can we say that? Explain in Japanese.

the two： _____　✑段落構成（3点）

なぜそのように言えるのか： _____　✑論理（9点）

_____

_____

4. Translate the following into Japanese: (3)That puts children who eat a lot of them at risk of obesity. Be sure to make "them" clear.　✑知識・技能（10点）

_____

5. The phrase which best suits for ☐X☐ is ☐.　✑論理（7点）

　a. As a result　　　b. At last　　　c. In addition　　　d. On the other hand

6. Which statement best summarizes the text?　✑全体把握（7点）

　a. Children in low- and middle-income countries are facing a different kind of problem from the past one.

　b. Cheap foods contain little nutrition, and this increases the number of children underweight.

　c. It is a good trend that the number of underweight children has been decreasing in low- and middle-income countries.

　d. The number of overweight children in developed countries is still too high, and this is a serious problem we need to solve.

1 People often ask which is the most difficult language to learn. This question is not easy to answer because there are many factors to *take into consideration. *In the first place, people learn their first language naturally, so the question is only asked when people learn a second language.

5 **2** First, (1)learners' first language can affect learning a second language. For example, a native speaker of Spanish will find *Portuguese much easier to learn than a native speaker of Chinese. This is because Portuguese is very similar to Spanish, while Chinese is very different. It is easier to learn a language which has similar *characteristics and rules to one's first language. Many people think 10 that Chinese is the hardest language to learn, possibly because they think that learning the Chinese writing and sound system is very difficult. However, for Japanese speakers, learning the Chinese writing system will be less difficult than for speakers of languages using the Roman alphabet because Japanese people already use Chinese characters.

15 **3** (2)Some people may learn languages more easily, while others find it very difficult. Teachers and circumstances also *play an important role, as well as each learner's motivation. If people learn a language because they need to use it professionally, they often learn it faster than people who are studying a language without any *particular purpose.

20 **4** No language is easy to learn well, though languages which are related to our first language are easier. (3)Learning a completely different writing system is a huge challenge, but that does not *necessarily make one language more difficult than another. In the end, (4)it is impossible to say that there is one language that is the most difficult in the world.

---

take ... into consideration：…を考慮にいれる　　in the first place：まず第一に，そもそも　　Portuguese：ポルトガル語
characteristic：特徴　　play an important role：重要な役割を果たす　　particular：特定の
necessarily：必ずしも（…でない）

本文音声

1. According to the text, which of the following is true about language learning?

🗨 主題 （7点）

a. Each learner's motivation plays an important role in learning their first language.

b. In Europe, everyone succeeds in learning a second language.

c. Language learning is a simple process.

d. There's no one who has no trouble learning a second language.

2. Why does the writer say (1)learners' first language can affect learning a second language? Explain in Japanese.　　　　　🗨 段落構成 （7点）

_____

_____

3. As to (2)some people may learn languages more easily, while others find it very difficult, who are likely to be "some people" and who are likely to be "others"? Explain in Japanese.　　　　　🗨 段落構成 （各7点）

・容易に言語習得できる人：_____

・言語習得に難しさを感じる人：_____

4. If you add further information to paragraph 3, which of the following will be the best?

a. How to organize your learning space such as your desk　　🗨 段落構成 （7点）

b. The most difficult language to learn

c. Characteristics of teachers who can help learners learn better

d. Why learning a second language is important

5. Translate the following into Japanese: (3)Learning a completely different writing system is a huge challenge, but that does not necessarily make one language more difficult than another.　　　　　🗨 知識・技能 （7点）

_____

_____

6. Why does the writer conclude that (4)it is impossible to say that there is one language that is the most difficult in the world? Explain in Japanese.　　🗨 全体把握 （8点）

_____

_____

語数（速読目標時間）	関連教科	関連SDGs	得 点
296（3分）	情報	—	
制限時間			
20分			/ 50

1 Let me share two important points to help you know *whether the information is correct or not.

2 First of all, it is important to give up the thought that "a search will answer all of the questions in the world." There are many other sources of information
5 in the world besides the Internet. *Instead of trying to solve all your questions with information from the Internet, it is better to use the Internet as a *supplement or a starting point for your research. If you do not use the Internet with such an attitude, false information may *deceive you easily. If you do not go to the library or contact an expert, you will not learn really important things.

10 **3** It is (1)also important to have (2)the ability to read and understand long texts. If you do not have the ability to read long texts, you will not be able to understand what is written in them. (3)You will be *overwhelmed by their large number of words and regard the texts as true just because they are written in long sentences. A large amount of text does not always mean that the truth is
15 written correctly and in detail. When AI technology is used, it is possible to create long sentences with little *substance. A long text may seem *plausible at first. When you read carefully, however, it often *turns out to be a long text that *makes no sense at all. It is necessary to improve your reading skill by practicing reading books.

20 **4** Keep (4)these two points in mind and you will be able to avoid misinformation. If you understand the role of the Internet and try to read and understand the large amount of text, you will not be easily deceived by poor-quality contents.

---

whether ... or not：…かどうか　　instead of ...：…のかわりに, …ではなく　　supplement：補足　　deceive：…をだます
overwhelm：…を圧倒する　　substance：内容, 中身　　plausible：もっともらしい
turn out to be ...：…であるとわかる　　make sense：意味をなす

本文音声

1. Which of the following is the main point of paragraph 2? ➥ 主題 (7点)

   a. Going to the library and contacting an expert is better than searching on the Internet.

   b. Information from the Internet is always false.

   c. Information from the Internet is not always correct.

   d. You can find all you need to know through the Internet.

2. In paragraph 3, (1)also is used to ☐. ➥ 文章展開 (7点)

   a. introduce the writer's second important point

   b. show that both readers and the writer have to have the ability to read a long text

   c. say that information from the Internet and other sources is true

   d. suggest that reading both short and long texts is important

3. Why do you have to have (2)the ability to read and understand long texts? In order to have it, what does the writer want you to do? Explain in Japanese. ➥ 段落構成 (各7点)

なぜ必要か：_____

_____

筆者は何をしてほしいと思っているか：_____

_____

4. Translate the following into Japanese: (3)You will be overwhelmed by their large number of words and regard the texts as true. ➥ 知識・技能 (8点)

_____

_____

5. What are (4)these two points? Explain each of them in Japanese. ➥ 文章展開 (各7点)

  ・_____

  ・_____

語数（速読目標時間）	関連教科	関連SDGs	得 点
302（3分00秒）	家庭	1 NO POVERTY / 2 ZERO HUNGER	
制限時間			
20分			/ 50

1 Does a meal of fried *crickets and *marinated *worms sound tasty to you? (1)While insects are already considered a good source of protein in some parts of the world, they are not very popular worldwide. However, there are good reasons for eating insects instead of meat and fish.

5 **2** Insects are a good food source because (2)eating them produces much less waste than eating meat or fish. When we eat chicken or beef, we generally only eat the muscles and throw away the rest. As Figure 1 shows, the majority of a cricket's body can be used as food —— only one-fifth is wasted. On the other hand, with most other protein sources, such as fish, chicken, and cattle, much more of the animal is wasted. 10 Only about half of a salmon or a chicken is used as food, and less than half of a cow is used. This means the most of animal's body is thrown away.

Figure 1: Portion of animal we can eat (%)

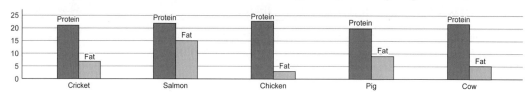

80% Cricket   50% Salmon   55% Chicken   55% Pig   40% Cow

3 Another reason for eating insects is that they are full of nutrition. For example, many insects are rich in protein. As illustrated in Figure 2, crickets have as much protein as salmon, chickens, and cows. They also contain less fat, so people can regard 15 them as a healthy choice. In addition, insects such as crickets are a good source of vitamins and minerals. They have 10 times as much vitamin B_{12} as salmon, almost five times as much magnesium as beef, and more calcium than milk.

Figure 2: Nutritional value of animal (grams per 100g of products)

	Cricket	Salmon	Chicken	Pig	Cow
Protein	~21	~21	~22	~20	~21
Fat	~7	~15	~3	~9	~6

4 It's clear that there are (3)benefits of replacing meat and fish with insects. In addition to being less wasteful and equally nutritious, insects are available all over the 20 world and they *reproduce rapidly. (4)As resources become *scarce and the global population increases, perhaps someday more people will consider sitting down for a meal of crickets and worms.

---

cricket：コオロギ   marinated：マリネ（料理）の   worm：イモムシ   reproduce：繁殖する   scarce：乏しい

本文音声

1. The writer mainly writes that ☐. 主題 (7点)

   a. eating insects seems unpleasant, so most people would avoid eating them

   b. eating insects will become a more common choice if we consider its merits

   c. we have to eat insects because it costs too much to grow animals for food

   d. we must stop eating animals because their numbers have been decreasing

2. (1)While can be replaced with ☐. 知識・技能 (7点)

   a. As long as   b. Because   c. Though   d. When

3. Why can we say (2)eating them produces much less waste than eating meat or fish?

Explain in Japanese with some examples. 段落構成 (7点)

_____

_____

4. According to the article and Figure 2, which of the following statements are true?

Choose two options. The order does not matter. 情報整理 (各3点)

   a. As a source of magnesium, beef is not as good as crickets.

   b. Both crickets and chicken are good sources of protein, vitamins, and minerals.

   c. Chicken contains richer protein than crickets while it contains less fat.

   d. Salmon contains nearly half as much vitamin B_{12} as crickets.

   e. Salmon is a far better source of protein than crickets.

5. What are the three (3)benefits of replacing meat and fish with insects? Explain in

Japanese. 文章展開 (各5点)

  •_____

  •_____

  •_____

6. Translate the following into Japanese: (4)As resources become scarce and the global

population increases, perhaps someday more people will consider sitting down for a

meal of crickets and worms. 知識・技能 (8点)

_____

_____

Lesson

10

語数(速読目標時間)	関連教科	関連 SDGs		得　点
332(3分20秒)	—	4 QUALITY EDUCATION	9 INDUSTRY, INNOVATION AND INFRASTRUCTURE	
制限時間				
20分				/ 50

1 Students who go to school in Talladega *County, Alabama, are given a laptop or a tablet. They use these devices in class and take them home at the end of the day. But Talladega County is in a *rural part of Alabama. Many students live in small towns or in the countryside. The towers and underground
5 cables that provide Internet access don't always reach these areas. In some homes, it's impossible to access the Internet.

2 Experts have a name for this situation. They call it the "(1)homework gap," because it's difficult for some students to do homework that *requires them to get online. "When you go home at the end of the day, you cannot access the
10 same information and technology tools as some of your classmates. That's the homework gap," said Beth Holland. She works at the *Consortium for School Networking.

3 (2)The homework gap isn't a problem only in Talladega County. According to a Pew Research Center study, about one in five homes with school-age kids
15 doesn't have high-speed Internet access. And 17% of teens say that *lack of good Internet access sometimes means they can't do their homework. "Kids are *excluded from learning *opportunities," Holland says.

4 Children across the country have found (3)creative ways to close the homework gap. In some school libraries, students can borrow mobile hot spots. Students in
20 several communities have created Wi-Fi maps. (4)Those let kids know about local businesses which provide the Internet to their customers, for example, cafés.

5 Talladega County created "(5)rolling study halls." Many students ride the bus to and from school each day along country roads. The average ride each way is an hour. Some are as long as 90 minutes. In 2018, wireless Internet was
25 installed on six school buses with long routes in rural areas. Now students can do homework during their daily rides. A teacher *comes along to help. "It has been a *game changer," Vicky Ozment, an officer for Talladega County Schools says. "It *leveled (6)the playing field."

county：郡　　rural：田舎の　　require ... to ～：…に～するよう要求する　　consortium：コンソーシアム(共同体)
lack：不足，欠乏　　exclude：…を排除する　　opportunity：機会　　come along：いっしょに来る
game changer：ゲームチェンジャー(物事の状況を一変させる人やアイディア)　　level：…を同じレベルにする，等しくする

本文音声

1. Explain the (1)homework gap in Japanese. 　　　　　　　　　　　　　　✎ 主題 (6点)

_____

_____

2. According to the text, Beth Holland would agree with the idea that ☐.　　✎ 意見 (5点)

　　a. the homework gap has both advantages and disadvantages

　　b. students should be given equal chances to study

　　c. teachers should stop giving homework online

　　d. we should consider the value of homework

3. The writer says (2)the homework gap isn't a problem only in Talladega County in order

　　to ☐.　　　　　　　　　　　　　　　　　　　　　　　　✎ 文章展開 (5点)

　　a. gather the opinions of some researchers

　　b. introduce the situation in other areas

　　c. point out other problems in Talladega County

　　d. say the homework gap is not a serious problem

4. What are the two (3)creative ways to close the homework gap? Explain in Japanese.

　　　　　　　　　　　　　　　　　　　　　　　　　　　　✎ 段落構成 (各5点)

　　• _____

　　• _____

5. Translate the following into Japanese: (4)Those let kids know about local businesses

　　which provide the Internet to their customers. Be sure to make "those" clear.

　　　　　　　　　　　　　　　　　　　　　　　　　　　✎ 知識・技能 (6点)

_____

6. What is (5)rolling study halls? Explain in Japanese with its purpose.　✎ 段落構成 (6点)

_____

7. What is (6)the playing field in this context? Explain in Japanese.　　✎ 論理 (7点)

_____

8. Vicky Ozment regards rolling study halls as a game changer because ☐.

　　a. it allows more students to use the school bus　　　　　　✎ 未知語 (5点)

　　b. it closes the homework gap by making good use of students' long rides to

　　　　and from school

　　c. students will not have trouble accessing the Internet even at home

　　d. teachers can help students learn even after school

1   Imagine this.   In a hot room with no windows, young women are working side by side.   The number of women working inside is too large to count.   They are workers in a factory in Bangladesh.   Factories like this one are called "sweatshops." The women are making jackets.   They must sew more than 1,000
5   jackets a day.   Each of them will take home just $3 for a whole day of work.   One week later, these same jackets will arrive in your country.   You won't have to pay a lot of money to buy them.   They are one example of (1)fast fashion.

2   When we say "fast fashion," we are talking about clothes that are made quickly and then sold at very low prices.   (2)These clothes cost so little that many
10   people can buy new ones easily —— and then throw them away when they *go out of style.   Over 150 billion new pieces of clothing are made every year!

3   Fast fashion may have some benefits for consumers, but it also has (3)a dark side.   Today, millions of people work in "sweatshops."   Many of these people live in developing countries.   They earn just a few dollars a day.   In these factories, it
15   is easy to get sick or get hurt.   Workers in the clothing industry often must use dangerous chemicals to create clothes.   It is clear that these chemicals are harmful to their health.   *To make matters worse, they can't take a rest when they feel sick.   If they miss a day because they are sick, they might lose their job.

4   On April 24, 2013, the Rana Plaza factory building in Bangladesh collapsed.   On
20   that day, many people learned for the first time how their clothes were made.   The factory had too many floors, too many workers, and too many machines.   (4)This accident killed and injured thousands of workers.   After the accident, many big clothing companies promised to do things differently.   They trained two million workers on how to work safely.   They brought in engineers to check their factories.

25   **5**   People are starting to see this negative side of fast fashion.   They are learning more about where their clothes come from.   In addition, the clothing industry is starting to respond.   (5)Some companies are creating clothes out of recycled or *organic fabrics, and others are encouraging customers to recycle their clothing.   (6)Everyone must play a part.   Learn more and think carefully
30   about your clothes.   It can make a real difference.

---

go out of style：流行遅れになる   to make matters worse：さらに悪いことに   organic fabric：有機生地

本文音声

1. As to the phrase (1)fast fashion, we use the word "fast" because ☐.　　✎主題 (7点)

   a. they are produced in large numbers and made rapidly and cheaply

   b. they are transported by a faster transportation

   c. they can be worn out faster than expensive clothes　wear … out：…をすり減らす

   d. we can put on them faster than other clothes thanks to their design

2. Translate the following into Japanese: (2)These clothes cost so little that many people can buy new ones easily —— and then throw them away when they go out of style.

                                                     ✎知識・技能 (8点)

_____

_____

3. Choose the examples of (3)a dark side. You may choose more than one option.

   a. Dangerous chemicals used to make clothes　　b. High taxes on clothes ✎情報整理 (10点)

   c. Low pay for the workers　　　　　　　　　　d. Not giving workers good rest

   e. Poor conditions that may make workers sick　　f. Poor sales of clothes

   g. Rising prices of fabrics　　　　　　　　　　h. Risks of getting injured or being killed

4. Describe (4)this accident in detail in Japanese.　　✎文章展開 (9点)

_____

_____

5. Translate the following into Japanese: (5)Some companies are creating clothes out of recycled or organic fabrics, and others are encouraging customers to recycle their clothing.　　✎知識・技能 (8点)

_____

_____

6. By saying (6)everyone must play a part, the writer wants us to ☐.　　✎意見 (8点)

   a. buy more fast fashion products in order to support the workers in developing countries

   b. keep in mind that the workers may be working in bad conditions before we buy

   c. stop buying fast fashion clothes because dangerous chemicals are used

   d. take part in a movement to help poor people in developing countries

1 Human being cannot live without water. In addition to drinking and washing, it also supports us economically through its *agricultural and industrial use. People in developed countries *take water for granted, but (1)this is not the case in developing countries. In those countries, water resources are
5 limited because of *droughts and other factors. There, children walk several hours every day to get water. They cannot go to school. The water they get is often dirty and unfit for drinking. (2)Is this a problem only in developing countries? In fact, developed countries are making water *shortages in developing countries more serious.

10 **2** Here is one concept of water consumption: "virtual water." Virtual water is water that we consume indirectly through the goods we import from other countries. For example, suppose you buy 100 grams of imported beef at the supermarket in Japan. To produce 100 grams of beef in Japan, 2,060 liters of water is required: water for the cows to drink, water for washing them, and water
15 for growing the grass and grain to feed them. Therefore, by importing beef from a foreign country, Japan is also indirectly consuming that country's water resources. (3)Food consumption in developed countries with low food *self-sufficiency depends on the water resources of other countries. In some countries, water shortages are becoming serious because they have to grow
20 crops and export them to developed countries.

3 Japan relies on imports for much of its food. (4)What can we do to improve the world's water situation? One way is to increase food self-sufficiency in Japan. As we produce more food *domestically, we can import less. This will reduce the total amount of virtual water. Another solution is to provide
25 technical assistance to developing countries with serious water shortages. By providing technology to build *wells or *convert seawater into fresh water, the quantity and quality of water to grow crops in developing countries will increase and improve.

4 There are also things we can do as consumers. Each one of us can try to
30 choose domestically produced foods. This will lead to an increase in food self-sufficiency. We can also grow our own vegetables in the garden. Enjoying fresh and delicious food will help solve the world's water problems.

本文音声

1. Which of the following is **not** true according to the text?　　🔊主題 (8点)

   a. Developed countries are related to the water shortages in developing countries.

   b. People in developed countries cannot help developing countries solve their water problems.

   c. Producing beef requires large amounts of water.

   d. Water problems also affect children's education in developing countries.

2. Choose the best option that paraphrases (1)this is not the case in developing countries.　　🔊論理 (8点)

   a. People in developing countries do not have easy access to water.

   b. People in developing countries know how to get enough water.

   c. People in developing countries do not think water shortages are a big problem.

   d. People in developing countries do not use water for agricultural and industrial use.

3. The writer says "(2)Is this a problem only in developing countries?" in order to ☐.

   a. show the other problems happening in developing countries　　🔊論理 (8点)

   b. tell readers that the same problems are happening even in developed countries

   c. suggest that developed countries are also responsible for the problem

   d. say that water shortages are going on all over the world

4. Translate the following into Japanese: (3)Food consumption in developed countries with low food self-sufficiency depends on the water resources of other countries.

   🔊知識・技能 (10点)

   _____

   _____

5. What are the answers to the question "(4)What can we do to improve the world's water situation?" Complete the table below in Japanese.　　🔊文章展開 (各4点)

国レベルで できること	・ ・
個人レベルで できること	・ ・

語数（速読目標時間）	関連教科	関連 SDGs	得 点
296(3分)		13 CLIMATE ACTION　15 LIFE ON LAND	
制限時間	地理歴史		
20分			/ 50

1　Plants and trees protect us in many ways.　They fight the climate change that causes *disastrous problems all over the earth.　They filter the air that we breathe, *absorb harmful chemical gases from the environment, and produce oxygen.　Also, they support the *diversity of flowers and animals.　They provide
5　us with food, shelter, and countless other benefits.　*Besides, they control and manage the effects of sun, wind, and rain.

2　The loss of forests can contribute to climate change, *desertification, *soil erosion, fewer crops, flooding, and increased greenhouse gases in the atmosphere.　One of the most dangerous and troubling effects of *deforestation
10　is the loss of animal and plant species due to their habitat loss.　Seventy percent of land animal and plant species live in forests.　(1)Deforestation threatens not only species known to us, but also those that are still unknown.　The loss of forests has an immediate and direct effect on their lives.　Unfortunately, (2)people who live in the highly industrialized parts of the world will never fully realize
15　the benefits we get from forests.

3　However, researchers who are taking (3)this issue very seriously have encouraged us to take the necessary steps to save trees.　For example, deforested areas have been replanted with new trees.　Apart from that, (4)we are going digital so that we can save paper and reduce the number of trees that are cut
20　down.　Also, we should educate our children about trees and encourage them to pass this knowledge on to their friends and *acquaintances.　The least that we can do is to grow plants in our garden and encourage our neighbors (5)to do the same.　Finally, governments can play an important role by making strict laws to punish people who *illegally cut down trees for their own benefit or without
25　permission.

disastrous：悲惨な　　absorb：…を吸収する　　diversity：多様性　　besides：その上
desertification：砂漠化　　soil erosion：土壌侵食　　deforestation：森林破壊　　acquaintance：知り合い
illegally：違法に

本文音声

1. According to the article, plants and trees are beneficial to us because they ____.

情報整理 (6点)

a. absorb harmful chemicals such as oxygen　　b. control the effects of the climate

c. have a relaxing effect　　　　　　　　　　　d. protect us from dangerous animals

2. Translate the following into Japanese: (1)Deforestation threatens not only species known to us, but also those that are still unknown.　　　知識・技能 (9点)

_____

_____

3. Which of the following has the closest meaning to (2)people who live in the highly industrialized parts of the world will never fully realize the benefits we get from forests?　　　知識・技能　段落構成 (6点)

a. People living in big cities do not know the advantages of forests at all.

b. People living in big cities have no idea about the importance of forests.

c. People living in developed countries are not aware of all the benefits that forests bring.

d. People living in developed countries are not interested in forests.

4. What is (3)this issue? Write in one word from the passage.　　　指示語 (8点)

_____

5. What is the meaning of (4)we are going digital?　　　未知語 (7点)

a. Companies producing digital devices are becoming popular.

b. More and more people are becoming like robots.

c. More and more people have learned how to use digital devices.

d. More and more people tend to be interested in mathematics.

6. What does (5)to do the same mean? Write in three words from the passage.

指示表現 (7点)

_____

7. Which of the following is **not** written in the passage?　　　全体把握 (7点)

a. Some deforested areas are replanted.

b. The negative effects of deforestation have been studied for hundreds of years.

c. We should save trees since they play a very important role in our lives.

d. We should tell the importance of forests to the future generations.

Lesson
14
語数（速読目標時間）　関連教科　関連SDGs　得　点
321（3分10秒）
7 AFFORDABLE AND CLEAN ENERGY
11 SUSTAINABLE CITIES AND COMMUNITIES
制限時間　　　　　　—
20分　　　　　　　　　　　　　　　　　　　　/ 50

1 The world's population is growing and demand for electricity is increasing. About 60% of the world's electricity demand is *generated by *thermal power. Nuclear power and water power are also known as major power sources. (1)Today, since more people have become aware of global problems like climate change, clean power generation methods have been introduced in many parts of the world. Here is an example of one such method in a Spanish city.

2 There are many orange trees in *Seville, Spain. The city is famous for the pleasant smell of oranges. In fact, however, the fruit of these oranges is too sour to be eaten. Therefore, they are often used to make *marmalade. However, most of them fall to the ground and become dangerous for *pedestrians, bike riders and cars. *Crushed oranges attract unpleasant insects and of course cause garbage problems. In order to deal with (2)these problems, a project has been started to (3)generate electricity from these oranges.

3 First, juice is taken from oranges and *fermented. The fermenting juice produces *methane gas. It is used to power an electric generator and generate clean electricity. In a trial run, 50kWh of clean energy was generated from about 1,000 kilograms of oranges. There are (4)two additional advantages. The orange *peels are reused as *fertilizer, so there is no waste. The creation of new jobs for this project, such as picking up fallen oranges, will also be a great benefit to the city.

4 At present, the city plans to use the electricity generated from oranges to run the city's *water treatment plant. In the future, the city plans to recycle all of its fallen oranges. If the project is successful, about 73,000 households will be able to receive electricity. (5)Clean electricity will be delivered to a clean city. It is no longer a dream.

5 Fallen oranges were once a "*nuisance" in the city. They are now changing into electricity to benefit people's lives.

---

generate：…を生み出す　　thermal power：火力発電　　Seville：セビリア（スペインの都市）
marmalade：マーマレード　　pedestrian：歩行者　　crush：…を押しつぶす　　ferment：…を発酵させる
methane：メタン　　peel：皮　　fertilizer：肥料　　water treatment plant：浄水場
nuisance：やっかいもの

本文音声

1. Translate the following into Japanese: (1)Today, since more people have become aware of global problems like climate change, clean power generation methods have been introduced in many parts of the world. ⌇ 知識・技能 (8点)

_____

2. What are (2)these problems? Explain in detail in Japanese. ⌇ 指示語 (8点)

_____

3. Explain how to (3)generate electricity from these oranges in Japanese. ⌇ 段落構成 (8点)

_____

4. What are (4)two additional advantages of this project?　Write both of them in Japanese. ⌇ 段落構成 (各5点)

• _____

• _____

5. Which of the following has the closest meaning to (5)clean electricity will be delivered to a clean city? ⌇ 文章展開 (8点)
   a. A beautiful city will send eco-friendly electricity to other areas or countries.
   b. Electricity which is generated without causing pollution will be used in a beautiful city.
   c. Electricity which does not contain harmful substances will be used in a sustainable city.
   d. The dirty city will clean the streets with electricity which is generated without nuclear power.

6. Which of the following best describes the content of the passage? ⌇ 全体把握 (8点)
   a. As the world population grows, the number of power plants has also been increasing.
   b. Seville has traditionally used clean energy to generate electricity.
   c. Oranges should be used worldwide to generate electricity.
   d. The power generation method in Seville solves several local problems at the same time.

1 When a group wants to make a decision, *the majority rule is usually preferred. This method has been widely used in modern *parliamentary and *Supreme Court decisions. It has existed since ancient times, and was (1)even used in the voting method of ancient Rome. We have long regarded the majority rule as an effective method of
5 decision-making. However, the majority rule is sometimes not the best method of *democratic decision-making. (2)In the majority rule, the option that receives the most votes is chosen, and the opinions of those who liked other options are ignored. In fact, the result of a majority rule sometimes differs from the true opinion of the group.

2 Imagine, for example, that you are in a group of 10 friends who are going out for
10 dinner. You decide what to have for dinner by the majority rule.

	Sushi	Yakiniku	Pizza
Total	**4 points**	**3 points**	**3 points**

In this case, you would go for sushi. However, (3)*what if all six of you who chose yakiniku and pizza do not want to eat sushi? The number of people who don't want to eat sushi is greater than that of those who want to eat sushi.

3 A more *satisfactory decision-making method than the majority rule is called
15 (4)*the borda rule. Each choice is given a score, and the total scores are compared. In this case, each person gives 3 points to the food they most want to eat and 1 point to the least.

	A	B	C	D	E	F	G	H	I	J	Total
Sushi	3	3	3	3	1	1	1	1	1	1	18
Yakiniku	1	2	2	2	3	3	3	2	2	2	22
Pizza	2	1	1	1	2	2	2	3	3	3	20

Following this result, you would go out for yakiniku. This method of decision-making is more democratic than the majority rule, since the *minority opinion is also reflected.
20 However, (5)this method also has a disadvantage. It requires more time to vote and to count the votes as the number of participants and options increases.

4 We have seen that the majority rule is not the most appropriate method of decision-making in every situation. However, it has the advantage of being easier to *carry out than other voting methods. The borda rule mentioned above may be a
25 more democratic method, but it is not practical in a nationwide election, for example. We should choose appropriate decision-making method *on the basis of the time and place.

本文音声

the majority rule：多数決　　parliamentary：議会の　　Supreme Court：最高裁判所　　democratic：民主的な
what if ... ：…だったらどうか　　satisfactory：満足できる　　the borda rule：ボルダ投票
minority：少数派　　carry out ... ：…を実行する　　on the basis of ... ：…にもとづいて

1. The word (1)even in paragraph 1 is used to ▢.　　　　🖙 知識・技能 (5点)

  a. give an example of another voting method

  b. say that the writer was proud of knowing the truth

  c. deny the thing the writer just said

  d. introduce a surprising fact

2. Translate the following into Japanese: (2)In the majority rule, the option that receives the most

  votes is chosen, and the opinions of those who liked other options are ignored. 🖙 知識・技能 (8点)

_____

3. As to (3)"what if all six of you who chose yakiniku and pizza do not want to eat sushi?", why

  does the writer need to write about such a case? Explain in Japanese.　　🖙 論理 (8点)

_____ 場合を例示するため。

4. What is (4)the borda rule? Explain in about 50 letters in Japanese.　　🖙 内容理解 (9点)

ボルダ投票とはどのようなものか：																						
															50							

5. The writer says (5)this method also has a disadvantage. What is the disadvantage? Explain

  in Japanese. Be sure to make "this method" clear.　　🖙 主題 (7点)

_____

6. Each sentence below (①〜③) explains some features of decision making. Choose the

  best option from the box below for each sentence.　　🖙 情報整理 (各2点)

  ① A leader makes an important decision without listening to others' opinions.　( )

  ② Most people accept this method as the preferable way in decision-making.　( )

  ③ Ideally it is a better method in democratic elections. *ideally「理想的には」　( )

  | a. the majority rule　　b. the borda rule　　c. other decision-making method |

7. Which of the following is closest to the writer's opinion?　　🖙 主題 (7点)

  a. It is good that the majority rule has been used since ancient times.

  b. It is surprising that the majority rule is widely used in modern societies.

  c. The best decision-making method differs according to the situation.

  d. The borda method is the most efficient method in this modern and democratic

    society.

Lesson

16

語数（速読目標時間）	関連教科	関連 SDGs	得 点
300(3分)			
制限時間	公民		
20分			/ 50

1 In Britain, (1)making both Saturdays and Sundays official weekend holidays from work is actually a *relatively modern concept. Before the 19th century, most workers did not have any days off. Throughout the 19th century, the British government slowly reduced working hours in factories and gave workers
5 more *breaks. There were also campaigns for official weekend holidays by travel companies and *labor unions. The campaigns began in 1840s. And by the end of the 19th century, many workers enjoyed Saturday afternoon and all of Sunday off from work.

2 (2)*Religious groups, entertainment companies, and workers all soon started
10 to see Saturday afternoon as an *advantageous break in the working week. For example, many religious leaders thought that these Saturday afternoons would refresh the *workforce and increase the number of people attending church on Sundays. Labor unions *urged workers to use these Saturday afternoons to educate themselves so that they could then get better jobs. The travel and
15 entertainment companies viewed the free Saturday afternoons as a business *opportunity. Train operators reduced fares for day trips to the countryside on Saturday afternoons. Theaters and music halls also began holding their main entertainment on Saturday afternoons. However, (3)perhaps the most influential event that created the modern weekend was the decision to have football
20 matches on Saturday afternoons. Watching football soon became an important part of the British weekend for many workers.

3 Because of (4)all the factors listed above, Saturday afternoons off became very popular. In fact, they were so popular that the weekend was eventually *extended to all of Saturday and Sunday in the 1930s.

25 **4** These days, the idea of decreasing the working week from five days to four days is getting support around the world. Many psychologists, economists, and employers now believe that a three-day weekend could help improve workers' *efficiency and health.

---

relatively：比較的　break：休憩　labor union：労働組合　religious：宗教の　advantageous：有利な，好都合な
workforce：労働者[力]　urge ... to ～：…に～するよう促す　opportunity：機会　extend：…を延長する
efficiency：効率

本文音声

1. Translate the following into Japanese: (1)making both Saturdays and Sundays official weekend holidays from work. 知識・技能（7点）

_____

2. According to the fact written in paragraph 1, ☐. 段落構成（7点）
   a. British people had no official holidays in the 18th century
   b. people worked after taking rest in the morning on Saturdays in the late 19th century
   c. reducing working hours wasn't discussed until official weekend holidays were set up
   d. travel companies started campaigns in the middle of the 18th century

3. How did (2)religious groups, entertainment companies, and workers see Saturday afternoons as an advantageous break? Explain each case in Japanese. 文章展開（各5点）
   religious groups :_____

   _____

   entertainment companies :_____

   _____

   workers :_____

   _____

4. Translate the following into Japanese: (3)perhaps the most influential event that created the modern weekend was the decision to have football matches on Saturday afternoons. 知識・技能（7点）

   _____

   _____

5. Choose one option that is **not** included in (4)all the factors listed? 指示表現 論理（7点）
   a. People were encouraged to improve their skills or knowledge.
   b. Several companies regarded Saturdays as a chance to earn money.
   c. Some factories let workers take a rest during their working hours.
   d. Some popular performances were held on Saturday afternoons.

6. What is an idea about labor which has been discussed recently? Explain in Japanese.
   内容理解（7点）
   _____

語数(速読目標時間)	関連教科	関連SDGs	得点
333(3分20秒)	公民・理科		
制限時間			
20分			/ 50

1 (1)Plastics are amazing materials. They can be as tough as a *bulletproof vest or as flexible as a sandwich bag. Plastics are in everything from cars to clothes —— and they're often cheap to make. A total of about 8.3 billion metric tons of plastic have been produced. (2)That's nearly 1,400 times the weight of the Great

5 Pyramid of Giza. Some of that plastic is still in use. But about 5.8 billion metric tons have been *discarded —— about 970 Great Pyramids' worth.

2 All that plastic trash is a serious environmental issue. Only about 9 percent of plastic waste has been recycled. Another 12 percent has been burned. The remaining 79 percent lies in *landfills or in nature, and it takes a long time for

10 that plastic to break down.

3 (3)Plastic trash is found from the top of Mount Everest to the bottom of the ocean. Many animals mistake this trash for food. If these animals get full of plastic, they may become unable to eat real food and *starve. Plastic garbage in the oceans endangers birds, turtles and other wildlife.

15 **4** Big pieces of plastic aren't the only problem. Discarded plastic can break into tiny bits called (4)microplastics. Winds *scatter these microplastics far and wide. Ocean *currents can spread them throughout the sea. These *pollutants *accumulate inside animals. They also get into our food and drinking water. Each American is estimated to consume more than 70,000 pieces of microplastic

20 per year. Right now, no one knows the risk from (5)that.

5 Scientists have some ideas about how to clean up this problem. The ambitious Ocean Cleanup project *aims to fish plastic *debris from *the Great Pacific Garbage Patch. *Microbes or *mealworms that eat plastic might someday live in landfills, and new nanotechnology could help microplastics

25 break down in the environment.

6 But many of these ideas are still *far from practical. The best way to help Earth right now, researchers say, is to stop buying so much plastic —— and then throwing it out —— in the first place.

---

bulletproof vest：防弾チョッキ　　discard：…を捨てる　　landfill：埋立地　　starve：飢える，餓死する
scatter：…をまき散らす　　current：流れ　　pollutant：汚染物質　　accumulate：蓄積する
aim to ～：～することを目指す　　debris：破片
the Great Pacific Garbage Patch：太平洋ごみベルト(太平洋にある，海洋ごみの多い海域)　　microbe：微生物
mealworm：ミールワーム(ゴミムシダマシの幼虫)　　far from ...：…からほど遠い

本文音声

1. The writer says that (1)plastics are amazing materials because ____. 　段落構成（6点）

   a. 8.3 billion metric tons of plastic have been produced

   b. they can be made into both hard and soft materials

   c. they can be produced without spending any money

   d. they can be thrown away easily

2. Translate the following into Japanese: (2)That's nearly 1,400 times the weight of the Great Pyramid of Giza. Be sure to make "That" clear. 　知識・技能（7点）

_____

_____

3. The writer says (3)plastic trash is found from the top of Mount Everest to the bottom of the ocean to ____. 　段落構成（6点）

   a. illustrate the light weight of plastic that can be carried anywhere by winds

   b. inform readers that people take plastic goods with them everywhere

   c. let readers know that plastic is so useful that it can be found in extreme locations

   d. show that plastic waste causes trouble everywhere on this planet

4. What are (4)microplastics? How are they spread around the world? Explain in Japanese. 　キーワード（各6点）

microplastics とは何か：_____

どのように広がるか：_____

5. What is (5)that? Explain in Japanese. 　指示語（7点）

_____

6. According to the text, which is the best action we should take to improve the situation? 　文章展開（6点）

   a. Stop going shopping so often.

   b. Take part in the Ocean Cleanup project.

   c. Try to avoid choosing goods using plastic.

   d. Wait for a new technology to be developed.

7. The best title for the text is ____. 　全体把握（6点）

   a. Bad Effects of Plastic Trash on the Environment

   b. How Humans Created Plastics that Damage the Environment

   c. How to Use Plastic Products Safely　　d. Our Future Living with Plastics

Lesson

18

語数（速読目標時間）	関連教科	関連 SDGs		得 点
327（3分20秒）	公民・保健体育	5 GENDER EQUALITY	10 REDUCED INEQUALITIES	
制限時間 20分				/ 50

1 (1)<u>Attractive female characters</u> frequently appear in South Korean dramas, and a great number of working women *identify with them. Many of the stories focus on ambitious heroines who are strong enough to protect the men they love. The heroines defeat typical *conservative men who are opposed to the

5　idea of women's participation in business. They also actively communicate with other women in local communities. Doing so can be a tough task, but they do it to get important information. The *principal male characters respect the heroines' ability and independence, and try to protect them so that their free lifestyle will not be *restricted.

10　**2** "One trend in recent South Korean drama series is that women's lives are presented *realistically through the stories," said Yone Yamashita, a professor of South Korean culture and women's studies. "Their creators write the stories with that in mind." (2)<u>This</u> is in contrast to *sentimental dramas which were popular among middle-aged or older women in the past, such as *Winter Sonata*.

15　**3** After the first entertainment boom in the 2000s ended, K-pop *reawakened interest in South Korean culture, mainly among Japanese teenagers, in the 2010s. In the latest boom, many people posting their drama reviews on social media are in their 20s to 40s. Of these, (3)<u>working women have a positive view of South Korean dramas</u>. They feel encouraged by the *decisive heroines.

20　**4** An award to honor *creations that contribute to gender equality was introduced in South Korea in 1999, and it encouraged these new types of dramas to enter the market. Working mothers, single-parent families, gender *inequality in households and other social issues, along with love affairs, are described in many such stories. "The dramas show a society a step ahead of

25　reality, and (4)<u>characters who break down walls that women frequently face appear in them</u>," said Yamashita. "Viewers can easily relate the problems in the dramas to their own, so the programs are supported by a wide range of viewers even in Japan."

---

identify with ...：…に共感する　　conservative：保守的な　　principal：主要な　　restrict：…を制限する
realistically：現実的に　　sentimental：感傷的な　　reawaken：目を再び覚まさせる　　decisive：決断力のある
creation：創作物　　inequality：不平等

本文音声

1. Which of the following is the best title of the passage? 主題 (7点)

   a. Differences between Korean and Japanese Dramas

   b. Why Korean Dramas Attract Viewers

   c. The Process of Making Korean Drama Series

   d. In Order to Break the Wall of Gender Discrimination in Korea

2. Choose **all** the (1)attractive female characters that appear in South Korean dramas.

   a. A female who depends on her partner or family    情報整理 (完答10点)

   b. A female who enjoys her own lifestyle

   c. A female who fights against gender equality in business

   d. A female who has good communication skills

   e. A female who is ambitious and decides her own actions

   f. A female who respects men's ability

3. What is (2)this? Explain in detail in Japanese. 指示語 (8点)

_____

4. Why do (3)working women have a positive view of South Korean dramas? Explain in Japanese. 文章展開 (9点)

_____

5. Translate the following into Japanese: (4)characters who break down walls that women frequently face appear in them. Be sure to make "them" clear. 知識・技能 (9点)

_____

6. Which of the following is closest to Professor Yamashita's opinion? 文章展開 (7点)

   a. The people who watch recent Korean dramas like to see women protected by men.

   b. Recent Korean dramas avoid describing gender inequality.

   c. The content of Korean dramas has not changed very much over the past 20 years.

   d. The creators have probably researched social issues to reflect them in their Korean dramas.

SDGs 関連語句特集

SDGs は，2015年9月の国連サミットで採択された「持続可能な開発のための2030アジェンダ」にて記載された2030年までに持続可能でよりよい世界を目指す国際目標です。17のゴールと169のターゲットから構成されています。ここでは，169のターゲットに使われる語句をピックアップしました。1.3や1.b などは，その単語が出現するターゲットを表します(アルファベットはターゲットを達成するための手段とされています)。

貧困をなくそう
End poverty in all its forms everywhere
あらゆる場所のあらゆる形態の貧困を終わらせる。

☐ **poverty** [pávərti] 名 「貧困，貧乏」
- ▶poor 形が the poor と冠詞をともなって名詞として使われる場合は「貧困層，貧しい人々」の意味。

☐ **vulnerable** [vʌln(ə)rəb(ə)l] 形 「傷つきやすい，脆弱な」1.3
- ▶be vulnerable to …「…を受けやすい，…に弱い」。
- ▶前出の the poor 同様に，冠詞 the をともなって使われるときはそのグループ(脆弱層)を指す。

☐ **property** [prápərti] 名 「財産」1.4
- ▶価値の有無にかかわらず所有しているものを表す。

☐ **inheritance** [ɪnhérɪt(ə)ns] 名 「相続」1.4
- ▶動詞は inherit [ɪnhérɪt]「…を相続する」。

☐ **resilience** [rɪzíljəns] 名 「強靭性」1.5
- ▶困難な状況から回復する強靭性を指し，近年はカタカナでも「レジリエンス」として使われる。
- ▶resilient 形は前出の vulnerable の対義語。

☐ **investment** [ɪnvés(t)mənt] 名 「投資」1.b
- ▶動詞は invest「…を投資する」。

☐ **eradication** [ɪrædəkéɪʃ(ə)n] 名 「撲滅」1.b
- ▶動詞は eradicate「…を撲滅する」。eradicate infectious diseases「感染症を撲滅する」。

飢餓をゼロに
End hunger, achieve food security and improved nutrition and promote sustainable agriculture
飢餓を終わらせ，食料安全保障及び栄養改善を実現し，持続可能な農業を促進する。

☐ **hunger** [hʌ́ŋgər] 名 「飢餓」
- ▶hungry は空腹の状態を表す形容詞。

- ▶hunger が動詞で使用される場合，for などをともない「熱望する」の意味になる。

☐ **nutrition** [n(j)u:tríʃ(ə)n] 名 「栄養」
- ▶nutritious 形は「栄養のある」(2.1)。
- ▶malnutrition 名「栄養不良」。

☐ **indigenous** [ɪndídʒənəs] 形 「先住の，土着の」2.3
- ▶indigenous peoples「先住民」と people が複数形で使われることが多い。複数の民族を表すため。

☐ **genetic** [dʒənétɪk] 形 「遺伝的な」2.5
- ▶genetically modified organism(GMO)「遺伝子組みかえ生物」。

☐ **diversity** [dɪvə́:rsəti] 名 「多様性」2.5
- ▶diversified 形「多様化された」。

☐ **cultivate** [kʌ́ltəvèɪt] 動 「…を栽培する」2.5
- ▶culture「文化」や agriculture「農業」と同じ語源。

☐ **equitable** [ékwətəb(ə)l] 形 「衡平な」2.5
- ▶fair and equitable「公正かつ衡平な」。fair「平等であること」に対し equitable は「つりあっている」。

☐ **livestock** [láɪvstàk] 名 「家畜」2.a
- ▶集合的な意味で使用される。The man raises livestock.「その男性は家畜を育てている。」

すべての人に健康と福祉を
Ensure healthy lives and promote well-being for all at all ages
あらゆる年齢のすべての人々の健康的な生活を確保し，福祉を促進する。

☐ **mortality ratio** [mɔ:rtǽləti réɪʃoʊ] 名 「死亡率」3.1
- ▶mortal [mɔ́:rt(ə)l] 形「死すべき，死を免れない」。

☐ **epidemic** [epədémɪk] 名 「伝染病の流行」3.3
- ▶pandemic [pændémɪk] は「世界的な大流行」。

☐ **hazardous** [hǽzərdəs] 形 「有害な」3.9
- ▶「危険な」と訳されることが多い。名詞形は hazard。dangerous よりかたい表現。

☐ **contamination** [kəntæmənéɪʃ(ə)n] 名 「汚染」 3.9
▶pollution に対し，異物が混入した際に起こる汚染の意味が含まれる。an oil contamination 「油分混入」。

質の高い教育をみんなに
Ensure inclusive and equitable quality education and promote lifelong learning opportunities for all
すべての人々への，包摂的かつ公正な質の高い教育を確保し，生涯学習の機会を促進する。

☐ **decent** [díːs(ə)nt] 形 「きちんとした」 4.4
▶decent jobs で「働きがいのある人間らしい仕事」とされている。通常「きちんとした，まともな」の意味で使用される。

☐ **literacy** [lít(ə)rəsi] 名 「読み書き能力」 4.6
▶literacy rate「識字率」。

☐ **numeracy** [n(j)úːm(ə)rəsi] 名 「基本的計算能力」 4.6

ジェンダー平等を実現しよう
Achieve gender equality and empower all women and girls
ジェンダーの平等を達成し，すべての女性と女児のエンパワーメントを図る。

☐ **gender** [ʤéndər] 名 「ジェンダー」
▶sex が生物学的な特徴を表すのに対し，gender は男，女，あるいはまったく別の性別として自身が理解している性別を表す。人間以外の生物に gender は使わない。

☐ **discrimination** [dɪskrìmənéɪʃ(ə)n] 名 「差別」 5.1
▶10.3に discriminatory 形「差別的な」もある。

☐ **exploitation** [èksplɔɪtéɪʃ(ə)n] 名 「搾取」 5.2
▶動詞は exploit [ɪksplɔ́ɪt]「…を搾取する」。

安全な水とトイレを世界中に
Ensure access to water and sanitation for all
すべての人々の水と衛生の利用可能性と持続可能な管理を確保する。

☐ **sanitation** [sæ̀nətéɪʃ(ə)n] 名 「衛生」
▶似た意味の hygiene [háɪʤìːn] 名「衛生」も6.2に出てくるが，sanitation が社会全体の清潔さを保つことに対し，hygiene は個人の健康を維持するためのもの。公衆衛生に関して hygiene は使用されない。

エネルギーをみんなにそしてクリーンに
Ensure access to affordable, reliable, sustainable and modern energy
すべての人々の，安価かつ信頼できる持続可能な近代的エネルギーへのアクセスを確保する。

☐ **renewable energy** [rɪn(j)úːəb(ə)l -] 名 「再生可能エネルギー」 7.2
▶太陽光，水力，風力などの自然の力で補充されるエネルギー。

☐ **fossil fuel** [fás(ə)l -] 名 「化石燃料」 7.a
▶石炭や石油など，化石となった有機物で燃料に使われてきたもの。エネルギーを取り出した後に排出される二酸化炭素などが環境問題として取り上げられているため，再生可能エネルギーの使用が世界的により注目を浴びている。

働きがいも経済成長も
Promote inclusive and sustainable economic growth, employment and decent work for all
包摂的かつ持続可能な経済成長及びすべての人々の完全かつ生産的な雇用と働きがいのある人間らしい雇用（ディーセント・ワーク）を促進する。

☐ **entrepreneurship** [àːntrəprənáːrʃɪp] 名 「起業」 8.3 (4.4)
▶フランス語源の entrepreneur に，英語の「地位」の意味の接尾辞 -ship が付いてできた語。

☐ **gross domestic product** 名 「GDP ＝国内総生産」 8.1
▶国内の市場で取引された物やサービスの付加価値の総計。

☐ **endeavor** [ɪndévər] 動 「図る」 8.4
▶「努力する」の意味。名詞も同じ形。

☐ **child labor** [- léɪbər] 名 「児童労働」 8.7
▶国際労働機関 (ILO) では，就業が認められる最低年齢は15歳以上と規定されている。

☐ **migrant** [máɪɡrənt] 形 「移住(性の)」 8.8
▶名詞もある。women migrants「女性の移住労働者」。
▶似た単語で immigrant [ímɪɡrənt] 名「移住者」

もあるが, migrant が「仕事やよりよい生活環境を求めてある場所から別の場所に移動する人」に対し, immigrant は「永住する目的で外国から移住してくる人」の意味。

 産業と技術革新の基盤をつくろう
Build resilient infrastructure, promote sustainable industrialization and foster innovation
強靱（レジリエント）なインフラ構築, 包摂的かつ持続可能な産業化の促進及びイノベーションの推進を図る。

□ **retrofit** [rétroʊfìt] 動 「…を改善する」 **9.4**
▶「新しい機能や部品を追加して改良する」の意味。

□ **respective** [rɪspéktɪv] 形 「能力に応じた」 **9.4**
▶「それぞれの」と訳されることが多い。同じように「それぞれの」の意味をもつ each と異なり複数形が続く。

□ **diversification** [dɪvə̀ːrsɪfəkéɪʃ(ə)n] 名 「多様化」 **9.b**
▶diversify の名詞形。

 人や国の不平等をなくそう
Reduce inequality within and among countries
各国内及び各国間の不平等を是正する

□ **inequality** [ìnɪkwálэti] 名 「不平等」
▶⇔ equality「平等」。

□ **disability** [dìsэbílэti] 名 「障害」 **10.2**
▶動詞は disable [dɪséɪb(ə)l]。disabled「障害のある」。

□ **ethnicity** [eθnísэti] 名 「民族(性)」 **10.2**
▶ethnic [éθnɪk] 形「民族の」。

□ **wage** [wéɪʤ] 名 「賃金」 **10.4**
▶毎月支払われる salary と違い, wage は時間や日にちごとに支払われる。

 住み続けられるまちづくりを
Make cities inclusive, safe, resilient and sustainable
包摂的で安全かつ強靱（レジリエント）で持続可能な都市及び人間居住を実現する

□ **urbanization** [э̀ːrbэnэzéɪʃ(ə)n] 名 「都市化」 **11.3**

▶**urban** [э́ːrbэn] 形「都市の」, urbanize [э́ːrbэnàɪz] 動「…を都市化する」。

□ **municipal** [mjʊnísэp(ə)l] 形 「都市の」 **11.6**
▶（市区町村など）地方自治体の。municipal high school「市立高校」。

□ **peri-urban** [pérэ-] 名 「都市周辺部」 **11.a**
▶接頭辞 peri- は「周りの」の意味。

 つくる責任つかう責任
Ensure sustainable consumption and production patterns
持続可能な生産消費形態を確保する

□ **retail** [ríːtèɪl] 名 「小売」 **12.3**
▶動詞「…を小売りする」, 副詞「小売りで」も同形。

□ **procurement** [prэkjʊэrmэnt] 名 「調達」 **12.7**
▶動詞は procure「…を調達する」。

□ **subsidy** [sʌ́bsэdi] 名 「補助金」 **12.c**

 気候変動に具体的な対策を
Take urgent action to combat climate change and its impacts
気候変動及びその影響を軽減するための緊急対策を講じる

□ **transparency** [trænspé(ə)rэnsi] 名 「透明性」 **13.a**
▶transparent 形「透明な」。

 海の豊かさを守ろう
Conserve and sustainably use the oceans, seas and marine resources
持続可能な開発のために海洋・海洋資源を保全し, 持続可能な形で利用する。

□ **the oceans, seas and marine resources** 「海洋・海洋資源」
▶ocean, sea, marine いずれも海を表す語であるが, ocean は「大洋」といった, sea よりも広い海を表す際に使われることが多い。sea はより一般的な「海」を表す語, marine は「海の」を意味する形容詞。

□ **debris** [dэbríː] 名 「ごみ」 **14.1**
▶「がれき, 破片」の意味のフランス語源の語。アクセント位置と語末の発音に注意。

□ **fishery** [fíʃэri] 名 「漁業」 **14.6**
▶「水産業, 漁場」の意味もある。

陸の豊かさも守ろう
Sustainably manage forests, combat desertification, halt and reverse land degradation, halt biodiversity loss
陸域生態系の保護，回復，持続可能な利用の推進，持続可能な森林の経営，砂漠化への対処，ならびに土地の劣化の阻止・回復及び生物多様性の損失を阻止する

☐ **desertification** [dìzəːrtəfəkéɪʃ(ə)n] 名 「砂漠化」
　▶desert [dézərt] 名「砂漠」, desertify [dɪzáːrtəfàɪ] 動「…を砂漠化する」。

☐ **terrestrial** [təréstriəl] 形 「陸域(の)」 15.1
　▶接頭辞 terr- は「土地の，地球の」の意味。territory「領土」。

☐ **deforestation** [dìːfɔ(ː)rɪstéɪʃ(ə)n] 名 「森林伐採」 15.2
　▶forestation「造林，植林」に反対の意味の接頭辞 de- が付いた形。

☐ **afforestation** [æfɔ̀ːrɪstéɪʃ(ə)n] 名 「植林」 15.2
　▶「…の方向へ」の意味の接頭辞 af- が付いた形。
　▶afforestation が不毛の地や荒廃した土地に新たに森を作ることを表すのに対し，forestation は，以前はあったが人間の利用により破壊された地域に樹木を植えること。

☐ **reforestation** [riːfɔ̀ːrɪstéɪʃ(ə)n] 名 「再植林」 15.2
　▶「再び」の意味の接頭辞 re- が付いた形。

☐ **poaching** [póʊtʃɪŋ] 名 「密猟」 15.7
　▶poach 動「…を密猟する」。

☐ **trafficking** [træfɪkɪŋ] 名 「(違法な)取引」 15.7
　▶traffic は「交通」の意味だが，動詞で使われると「(違法な)取引をする」の意味になることが多い。

☐ **flora and fauna** [flɔ́ːrə], [fɔ́ːnə] 名 「動植物」
　▶flora は「植物」, fauna は「動物」を集合的に表す語。

平和と公正をすべての人に
Promote just, peaceful and inclusive societies
持続可能な開発のための平和で包摂的な社会を促進し，すべての人々に司法へのアクセスを提供し，あらゆるレベルにおいて効果的で説明責任のある包摂的な制度を構築する。

☐ **torture** [tɔ́ːrtʃər] 名 「拷問」 16.2
　▶動詞でも使われ「…を苦しめる」。

☐ **illicit** [ɪlísɪt] 形 「違法な」 16.4
　▶illegal [ɪlíːg(ə)l] 形「違法な」は「法律に反した」の意味，illicit はそれに加え「道徳に反した」の意味をもつ。

☐ **corruption** [kərÁpʃ(ə)n] 名 「汚職」 16.5

☐ **bribery** [bráɪb(ə)ri] 名 「贈賄[収賄]行為」 16.5

パートナーシップで目標を達成しよう
Revitalize the global partnership for sustainable development
持続可能な開発のための実施手段を強化し，グローバル・パートナーシップを活性化する。

☐ **revenue** [révən(j)ùː] 名 「(国家の)歳入」 17.1

☐ **official development assistance** 名 「ODA ＝政府開発援助」 17.2
　▶開発途上地域の開発を目的とする政府及び政府関係機関による資金・技術提供などの国際協力活動。

☐ **debt** [dét] 名 「債務」 17.4
　▶「借金」の意味。発音に注意。

☐ **North-South, South-South, triangular** 「南北協力，南南協力，三角協力」 17.6
　▶North-South は先進国が途上国の開発の支援を，South-South は途上国間での支援を，そして三角協力は先進国が途上国間の開発を支援することを指す。

☐ **multilateral** [mÀltilǽt(ə)rəl] 形 「(多国間での)多角的な」 17.10

他の教科等に関連する語句特集

他の教科等で学習する内容を，英語を用いて課題解決することで，英語だけでなく，その内容に対する理解が深まります。ここでは，他の教科等で学習する内容を，学習指導要領などからピックアップしました。

国語　Japanese Language

- **Chinese character** [tʃàiníːz kǽrəktər] 名 「漢字」
  - ▶common Kanji「常用漢字」。
- **classic** [klǽsɪk] 名 「古典」
  - ▶classical Japanese literature とも表される。教科を表す際は classics（複数形）の形で表される。
- **colloquial** [kəlóʊkwiəl] 形 「口語の」
  - ▶「話し言葉の」。
- **literary** [lítərèri] 形 「文語の」
  - ▶「書き言葉の」。
- **context** [kántekst] 名 「文脈」
- **metaphor** [métəfɔ̀ːr] 名 「比喩」
  - ▶Life is a river.「人生は川のようだ。」のような，別のものに例えた表現。
- **euphemistic** [jùːfəmístɪk] 形 「婉曲的」
  - ▶I am between jobs.「失業中だ。」のような，遠まわしな表現。
- **rhetoric** [rétərɪk] 名 「修辞」
  - ▶豊かな表現をするための文章表現の総称で，上記 metaphor や euphemistic expression，inversion「倒置法」などが含まれる。

地理歴史　Geography and History

- **disaster** [dɪzǽstər] 名 「災害」
  - ▶台風や水害などの natural disaster や，人為的な原因によって起こる火事や事故を指す場合も使用される。an air disaster「航空機の大惨事」。
- **hazard map** [hǽzərd mǽp] 名 「ハザードマップ」
  - ▶「災害予想図」。自然災害による被害の軽減や防災対策に使用する目的で，被災想定区域や避難場所・避難経路などの防災関係施設の位置などを表示した地図。
- **topography** [təpágrəfi] 名 「地形図」
  - ▶等高線や色を使って高度や土地の形態を表す図。
- **modernization** [mὰdərnəzéɪʃ(ə)n] 名 「近代化」
  - ▶modernize 動「…を近代化する」。

- **popularization** [pὰpjələrəzéɪʃ(ə)n] 名 「大衆化」
  - ▶popularize 動「…を大衆化する」。
- **material** [mətí(ə)riəl] 名 「資料」

公民　Civics

- **sovereignty** [sáv(ə)rənti] 名 「主権」
  - ▶sovereignty of the people「国民主権」。
- **productive age** [prədʌ́ktɪv -] 名 「生産年齢」
  - ▶生産活動に従事することのできる年齢。一般的に15歳〜64歳を指す。
- **voting** [vóʊtɪŋ] 名 「投票」
  - ▶election「選挙」。presidential election「大統領選」。
- **contract** [kántrækt] 名 「契約」
  - ▶上記の「投票」など，成人年齢引き下げにともない，18歳から親の同意なくできるようになったことの例に，（ローンや携帯電話などの）契約締結がある。
- **consumer** [kənsjúːmər] 名 「消費者」
  - ▶consume 動「…を消費する」。
- **security** [sɪkjʊ́(ə)rəti] 名 「安全保障」
  - ▶国家の安全保障について言うとき，特に national security と表記する場合もある。
- **EEZ** [íːíːzíː] 名 「排他的経済水域」
  - ▶Exclusive Economic Zone の略。
  - ▶領海（territorial sea）の外側，領海の基線から200海里（nautical miles）内で認められる主権的権利を持つ水域。
- **employment** [ɪmplɔ́ɪmənt] 名 「雇用」
  - ▶employ 動「…を雇用する」，employer 名「雇用主」，employee 名「従業員」。

数学　Mathematics

- **data analysis** [- ənǽlɪsɪs] 名 「データの分析」
  - ▶analysis「分析」。複数形は analyses [ənǽlɪsìːz]。
- **formula** [fɔ́ːrmjələ] 名 「公式」
  - ▶the formula for calculating distance「距離を計算する公式」
- **equation** [ɪkwéɪʒ(ə)n] 名 「方程式」
- **shape** [ʃéɪp] 名 「図形」
  - ▶「図形」全般を表す際は複数形で表される。

- ☐ **function** [fʌ́ŋkʃ(ə)n] 名 「**関数**」
  - ▶「関数」全般を表す際は複数形で表される。

理科　Science

- ☐ **observation** [àbzərvéɪʃ(ə)n] 名 「**観察**」
  - ▶observe 動「…を観察する」。知覚動詞で，ほかにも「…に気づく」「…を述べる」「…を遵守する」などの意味をもつ多義語である。
- ☐ **hypothesis** [haɪpáθəsɪs] 名 「**仮説**」
  - ▶複数形は hypotheses [haɪpáθəsìːz]。
- ☐ **phenomenon** [fɪnámənàn] 名 「**現象**」
  - ▶複数形は phenomena [fɪnámənə]。
- ☐ **particle** [páːrtɪk(ə)l] 名 「**粒子**」
- ☐ **mass** [mǽs] 名 「**質量**」
  - ▶物質の動きにくさ，慣性の大きさ。質量は地球上でも宇宙空間でも変わらない。単位は kg。
- ☐ **(aqueous) solution** [(éɪkwiəs) səlúːʃ(ə)n] 名 「**水溶液**」
  - ▶saturated aqueous solution「飽和水溶液」。
- ☐ **ecosystem** [íːkoʊsìstəm] 名 「**生態系**」
  - ▶太陽光のエネルギーを源とした，生物とそれらを取り巻く環境がお互いに関わり合う体系。

保健体育　Health and Physical Education

- ☐ **lifelong sport** [láiflɔ̀ːŋ -] 名 「**生涯スポーツ**」
  - ▶競うことよりも，生涯に渡って健康的な体を維持することを目的としたスポーツ。
- ☐ **first aid** [- éɪd] 名 「**応急手当**」
  - ▶first-aid の形で使用されることもある。
  - ▶形容詞としても使われる。first-aid kit「救急箱」。
- ☐ **cardiopulmonary resuscitation** [kàrdiəpúlmənəri rɪsÀsɪtéɪʃ(ə)n] 名 「**心肺蘇生法**」
  - ▶cardiopulmonary 形「心肺の」，resuscitation 名「蘇生」。
- ☐ **AED** 名 「**自動体外式除細動器**」
  - ▶Automated External Defibrillator の略。単に Defibrillator と呼ばれることもある。
- ☐ **lifestyle disease** [- dɪzíːz] 名 「**生活習慣病**」
  - ▶病気全般を表す際は複数形で表される。食事や運動，休養，喫煙，飲酒などの生活習慣が深く関与し，それらが発症の要因となる疾患の総称。

家庭　Home Economics

- ☐ **food, clothing and shelter** 名 「**衣食住**」
  - ▶necessities of life を「衣食住」と訳す場合もある。

- ☐ **welfare** [wélfèər] 名 「**福祉**」
- ☐ **consumption** [kənsʌ́mpʃ(ə)n] 名 「**消費**」
  - ▶consumption tax「消費税」。
- ☐ **household** [háʊshòʊld] 名 「**世帯**」

情報　Information

- ☐ **information moral** [- mɔ́ːrəl] 名 「**情報モラル**」
- ☐ **information literacy** [- lít(ə)rəsi] 名 「**情報リテラシー**」
  - ▶セキュリティや倫理的な問題を含む情報の処理能力を指すことが多い。
- ☐ **programming** [próʊɡræmɪŋ] 名 「**プログラミング**」
- ☐ **simulate** [símjəlèɪt] 動 「**…のシミュレーション[模擬実験]をする**」
- ☐ **big data** [- déɪtə] 名 「**ビッグデータ**」
  - ▶全体を把握することが困難な巨大なデータ群。

Sources

Lesson 2

Excerpts from *Amazing Chocolate* from Success with Reading 1 from Cosmos Culture Ltd. by Michelle Witte, Zachary Fillingham and Gregory John Bahlmann

Lesson 6

Excerpts from *Seriously Curious* from The Economist by Tom Standage